GRACE

encouraging • growing • releasi

MOVEMENT, PRAYER & SCRIPTURE

40 devotionals enabling you to begin a journey, build a foundation, and share your heart through dance and movement

ANNA GILDERSON

MOVEMENT, PRAYER & SCRIPTURE

40 devotionals to begin a journey, build
a foundation and share your heart
through dance and movement

ANNA GILDERSON

AUTUMN PEARL PUBLISHING

ISBN print – 978-1-7398401-2-9
eBook ISBN - 978-1-7398401-3-6

Book cover and layout by Spurwing Creative

Scripture quotations taken from The Holy Bible, New International Version® NIV®

Copyright © 1973 1978 1984 2011 by Biblica, Inc.™

Used by permission. All rights reserved worldwide.

Autumn Pearl Publishing

CONTENTS

INTRODUCTION

This series is designed to help both the experienced mover and the non-mover to deepen their relationship with God, using dance and movement. My desire is that each day will offer you different chances to engage with movement and speak to and hear from God. Hopefully you will gain the confidence to try adding movement into your daily routine whilst exploring God's word.

Each day there will be a focal verse or verses. Sometimes they have been extracted and you will need to read the wider passage (it is clear when this needs to happen). The devotional is then broken down into three main sections:

Pause – This starts you thinking in response to the verse for the day. Sometimes it will be just questions; other times it will be what God wants to say to you through the verse.

Pray – This is a prayer prompt for you to use how you wish before you go further with the day's devotional.

Move – This suggests ways for you to initiate movement from the verse.

The final section – **Move it Further** – is a chance to develop movement deeper and will challenge you to interpret God's word further. You will also find a song suggestion and questions to use in your journal time to help you document the journey that you go on.

Over the course of the 40 days, there are five key areas the devotional series will cover:

- Ready Your Heart
- Hear God's Guidance
- Armour of God
- God's Truths
- The Journey of the Cross

Each area is designed to look at your journey of faith as a whole, recognising how you can be strong in movement but also in your conversation with God. God created every part of us, so we need to allow each part of us to flourish when it's needed.

Some tips before you get going:

- Identify the same time each day to focus on the devotional – this will help it to become a habit.
- Try different locations – inside and outside, for example. The effects of your movements might change.
- Why not ask others to join you? This series works well with groups as a warm-up or icebreaker at the beginning of your session.
- All Bible references come from the New International Version.
- To get the most from each day, I recommend setting aside at least 20 minutes. This will allow you to soak in the depth and breadth of each devotional.
- You are encouraged to keep a record in any way that suits you – a diary, drawings, photos, videos etc. This will help keep you motivated over the course of your journey, during the devotionals and after.
- Share with others what you discover. Everyone needs encouragement at some point. Offer that out to others through your experiences when you can.

One final thing: you will notice on some of the days, there is a word in bold in the Pause section. If you're struggling to work through the Scripture and the questions that day, this word can act as inspiration for you to go deeper with the Scripture.

Have fun as you explore and let God lead and develop your movement. Remember, there is no right or wrong way to explore His word. It is unique, just like you!

PART ONE
Ready Your Heart

Part one begins in the Psalms, looking at some key verses that can help ready our hearts and acknowledge the things that God has supported and can support us through.

DAY
1

He determines the number of the stars
and calls them each by name.

PSALM 147:4

PAUSE

Every star is different; they all have a purpose. This is how God made them and us. As you pause today, remember that you are **uniquely** made, created for a purpose and given a name that God treasures, loves and can't wait to see grow.

Just as God poured love into creating the world, He poured love into creating you - each part of your personality and how you walk through life. God wants you to shine. He wants you to know that He chose your name.

PRAY

Father God, help me to accept that I am unique, that there is only one of me. Father, lead me to a place where people see I shine for you. Amen.

MOVE

Standing still, imagine you are holding a star in your hands. Think about what size it might begin at and how big it could get. What happens as that star burns brighter? What does it do? How do you react?

Consider what you do if you touch something hot, look at something bright or get warm. There are two physical reactions normally – you can't stay still and your gestures and movements get bigger. What do you discover?

SONG SUGGESTION

'Burn Like a Star' by Rend Collective

MOVE IT FURTHER

Create a small sequence that expresses to you what it feels like to know you are unique. Think about the things you love to do, the feeling God's love brings and how you feel knowing that God wants you to shine bright. Combine that with your bigger and brighter star movements that you explored above and use this as a prayer dance.

JOURNAL

How has this verse impacted your dance and movement journey today?

- This happened when I moved…
- Thank you for…
- Please help me with…
- Inspiration came from…

DAY
2

My soul is weary with sorrow;
strengthen me according to your word.

PSALM 119:28

PAUSE

Take a moment to breathe. Inhale clean, calm air. Exhale those feelings of weariness. Inhale and know that God lifts you up in that breath, and when you exhale, know that God is taking that **weariness** away. Spend at least five minutes concentrating on your breathing.

Really focusing on the inhale through your nose, inflate your chest cavity and draw breath into every part. As you exhale through your mouth, concentrate on drawing your belly button in and back towards your spine. The longer you do it for the more relaxed your body will become.

PRAY

Father God, guide me to put pauses in my day where I can feel you strengthen me in those moments when I am on my knees. Flood my body as I breathe deeply, helping me to relax into your arms. Amen.

MOVE

On a piece of paper, write the things that are making you weary. Create a movement for each. Stand on the piece of paper, and as you do each movement, actively choose to breathe God's strength into the move and let Him take the burden as you breathe out.

SONG SUGGESTION

'Only Jesus' (Instrumental) by Bethel Music

MOVE IT FURTHER

What's the opposite of feeling weary? Develop a transition for each of your weary movements that takes you from the movement to a movement of strength.

This will help you activate a physical correlation between the weariness and knowing where God can take you, if you pause, breathe and allow Him the space to bring energy where you need it.

JOURNAL

How has this verse impacted your dance and movement journey today?
- This happened when I moved…
- Thank you for…
- Please help me with…
- Inspiration came from…

DAY
3

Look to the LORD and his strength;
seek his face always.

PSALM 105:4

PAUSE

Moments in our lives sneak up and take our focus away from God. God desires that we **seek** His face always, looking for His strength to lift us in those moments. Pause and think about your week so far. Where has God been in it? Have you chosen to seek Him and let Him help you when you've struggled? What is getting in the way of you seeking Him?

PRAY

Father God, help me to recognise when I am not looking to you for help. Please put a blocker in my way that will show me I need to change my course. Shine a light in those times when I'm not aware I am seeking you. Help me to realise how you are always there giving me strength when I need it. Amen.

MOVE

If you were looking for God – seeking Him out – what would that look like in a dance or movement? Consider whether you stay still, move about, are animated or subdued. Piece together some movements as if you are going on a journey.

SONG SUGGESTION

'I See You' by Chris Tomlin, Brandon Lake

MOVE IT FURTHER

Try picking up something heavy from the ground. Where does your strength come from, and how do you need to position your body? Let me walk you through one way to explore this. Concentrating on your breathing, take nice, slow, deep breaths and imagine you were reaching down to pick something up. Focus on where you tense your muscles, your placement of weight, the muscles and body parts that you use to achieve this. Once you have explored this, consider how the use of strength, muscles and focus helped you achieve your aim. Apply these feelings to the movements that you explored earlier.

JOURNAL

How has this verse impacted your dance and movement journey today?
*   This happened when I moved…
*   Thank you for…
*   Please help me with…
*   Inspiration came from…

DAY
4

would not God have discovered it,
since he knows the secrets of the heart?

PSALM 44:21

PAUSE

Over the past week, what have you not spoken about? What have you kept **secret**? God knows where you go, what you think and speak. This means He also knows your dreams and desires – He sees inside your heart and wants the best for you.

Take a piece of paper and draw a big heart. Inside the heart, write those unspoken things, pausing and acknowledging them when it might have been hard to over the past week.

PRAY

Father God, you know the secrets I have, the ones that keep coming back; you know what the outcome will be. Please help me feel safe as I invite you in to lead me through it. Amen

MOVE

How do you receive a treasured possession? Imagine this…

You're waiting in a room and Jesus walks in. He hands you a box and tells you that in it is something that you will discover about yourself. The box is beautifully decorated with intricate wood carvings on the outside. But what will it be like on the inside? Spend some time creating movements that explore anticipation, opening, revealing and receiving. How do you accept what God wants you to discover about yourself?

SONG SUGGESTION

'Touch the Sky' by Instrumental Worship Project from I'm In Records

MOVE IT FURTHER

Write down one of your secrets/dreams/desires and cup it in your hands (or a small box if you happen to have one). Now imagine God giving it to you and you receiving it. What does your heart want to do? What do your movements do? Do you truly understand that God wants you to receive your dreams/desires?

JOURNAL

How has this verse impacted your dance and movement journey today?
- This happened when I moved…
- Thank you for…
- Please help me with…
- Inspiration came from…

DAY
5

He says, "Be still, and know that I am God;
I will be exalted among the nations,
I will be exalted in the earth."

PSALM 46:10

PAUSE

Where is your whirlwind happening at the moment? Where is your **stillness**? Stillness is not something to be afraid of; it brings clarity, purpose and breath. God wants you to explore His stillness; in that stillness, you can feel Him deeply. Have you given God any stillness this week? Or have you been in a whirlwind, rapidly moving from one place to another. Pause and acknowledge what you need to experience stillness. This doesn't have to be the physical action of being still; it could be recognition of things you enjoy that enable you to have stillness in your soul.

PRAY

Father God, I thank you that you calm the seas, that you bring peace in amongst turmoil. But Father, please help me to be still, so I see your glory on this earth. Help me to have the confidence in the things that I enjoy doing and the stillness you can bring my soul from them. Let me trust that your stillness helps me walk your path with more strength. Amen.

MOVE

Create a position of what it means to 'know that I am God'. Hold it for at least a minute, if not longer. Enjoy pausing, using the time to be still in God's presence, to rest. Then, when you're ready, step out into movements showing God's glory.

God's glory is something that is around us all the time, even when we don't recognise it. It's how He moves, talks, creates and shares.

SONG SUGGESTION

'Be Still' by Hillsong Worship

MOVE IT FURTHER

If you're able, step outside with a piece of fabric and hold it in the air. Watch what it does, how it moves, if it pauses in any way or creates shapes. Take up your 'know that I am God' shape using the fabric. Be still, holding it, then step out into the movements, showing God's glory. This time using the fabric as you move.

JOURNAL

How has this verse impacted your dance and movement journey today?

- This happened when I moved…
- Thank you for…
- Please help me with…
- Inspiration came from…

DAY 6

Surely, LORD, you bless the righteous;
you surround them with your favor as with a shield.

PSALM 5:12

PAUSE

God's love is all encompassing; it's above, below, to the left and to the right. He wants to **surround** us and protect us. If you are able to, take a moment to pause and step outside as you begin this devotional. Close your eyes and feel the air and surroundings around you. God's presence wants to surround you. That presence is like a shield that will encompass and carry you in the times you need it most. Helping to support you in the situations where God's righteousness needs to be at the centre of your life.

PRAY

Father God, I am sorry for those moments when I have not acted righteously. Help me to remember that in all circumstances you surround me and protect me. I thank you that your presence can calm anything that is going on. Amen.

MOVE

Create three or four strong movements, exploring the word 'surrounded'. When exploring a word, consider your feelings, its definition, what it could look like visually and how others see it.

Strong movements mean placing emphasis, tension and power in your actions. Think of catching something and then releasing it slowly. There is strength in that action, which enables you to deepen your movement and the resulting acknowledgement of how God surrounds us.

SONG SUGGESTION

'Peace Over You' by Here Be Lions

MOVE IT FURTHER

Reflect on a moment when you didn't act in God's best interest. Using the movements you created for the word 'surrounded', invite God into that situation and let God be in it with you.

JOURNAL

How has this verse impacted your dance and movement journey today?

- This happened when I moved…
- Thank you for…
- Please help me with…
- Inspiration came from…

DAY
7

My frame was not hidden from you
when I was made in the secret place,
when I was woven together in the depths of the earth.

PSALM 139:15

PAUSE

You were made with such love and intricacy; God lavished His time, **weaving** you into the way that you are. Do you believe God made *every* part of you?

As you begin today's devotion, make a note of the bits you love about yourself and the ones that you struggle with. The verse talks about the depths of the earth, the core. God weaved your core together too, so don't forget His design goes that deep as well!

PRAY

Father God, I thank you that I am woven together by you with love, care and purpose. Thank you for things that are woven into my life. Some I know already; many are still to be revealed. Please help me to let your love sink to the depths of my heart, into the very core. Amen.

MOVE

Using the following words as inspiration, explore how they can be put into movements.

- Hidden
- Frame
- Woven
- Love
- Purpose

This is an opportunity to really accept the meaning of this verse and allow your movements to become a prayer.

SONG SUGGESTION

'Don't Hide' (feat. Feranmi Oguns) by Lucy Grimble

MOVE IT FURTHER

Arrange the words into an order that suits you and apply this to the movements that you created. This is your starting sequence. Repeating the sequence, explore a variation of the original. This could be done by speed, level, size or accent.

JOURNAL

How has this verse impacted your dance and movement journey today?

- This happened when I moved…
- Thank you for…
- Please help me with…
- Inspiration came from…

PART TWO
Hear God's Guidance

God speaks to us all in different ways; in the busyness of life, it can be hard to focus on what He is saying and put it into action. As we enter Part Two, we take a moment to pause to remember how God's word can give us guidance, supporting us when life is difficult. Part Two is still in the Psalms – it's such a great book with so much content!

DAY 8

Teach me to do your will,
for you are my God;
may your good Spirit
lead me on level ground.

PSALM 143:10

PAUSE

Do you know what God's will is for you? Where He wants to lead you? The Holy Spirit is there as our guide and mentor to lead us through moments when the pathway is not clear and to keep us **level**. Pause and think about your journey of faith and your life currently. Does it feel like it is on level ground? Are you allowing the Holy Spirit to infiltrate your journey?

PRAY

Father God, thank you for giving us the Holy Spirit to help teach and guide us. Please help me identify the bits in my life where I am not letting you lead. I thank you that through you I can walk on level ground. Amen.

MOVE

Thinking about the pathway that you are on with your faith, create three movements: one low level, one medium level and one high level, choosing a level that matches a point on your pathway. These movements can be static (still) or you can choose to make them dynamic.

SONG SUGGESTION

'Champion' (Instrumental) by Worship Portal

MOVE IT FURTHER

As you become more familiar with your movements, practise changing between the three levels. Consider adding in a travelling movement between each level. How does your pathway grow? What does your pathway look like? If you now choose to invite and include the Holy Spirit on that pathway, how does it change?

JOURNAL

How has this verse impacted your dance and movement journey today?

- This happened when I moved...
- Thank you for...
- Please help me with...
- Inspiration came from...

DAY 9

Teach me your way, LORD,
that I may rely on your faithfulness;
give me an undivided heart,
that I may fear your name.

PSALM 86:11

PAUSE

Are you giving God your whole heart? God's faithfulness abounds in so many ways. Each day, take the time to acknowledge that **relying** on God is about learning to lean in and lean on Him.

Recognise the moments when He is faithful and consistent in being there for you.

PRAY

Father God, please help me shift my mindset so my whole heart is for you. Help me to realise that when I choose to trust your faithfulness, my way forward will be clear. Amen.

MOVE

Take two sheets of paper. On one piece, write what's dividing your heart/ what you are struggling with. On the other piece of paper, write down what faithfulness means to you. Place the two pieces of paper on the floor, with a large gap between them. How can you move from one to the other? This allows you to explore the action of moving from a place of division to a place where you can accept God's faithfulness.

SONG SUGGESTION

'Always Good' (Instrumental) by Lighthouse Piano

MOVE IT FURTHER

Create a shape for 'undivided heart' and another for 'faithfulness'. Explore creating the shape, travelling between the different pieces of paper and creating the other shape. Make a choice to do this for each thing that you feel is dividing your heart at the moment.

JOURNAL

How has this verse impacted your dance and movement journey today?

- This happened when I moved…
- Thank you for…
- Please help me with…
- Inspiration came from…

DAY
10

I will instruct you and teach you in the way you should go;
I will counsel you with my loving eye on you.

PSALM 32:8

PAUSE

Whatever you are struggling with today, God has got it; He is listening and always wants the best for you. He will provide **counsel** with a friend when you need it most. Part of following Christ requires us to have faith that God will lead us where we need to go and equip us with what we need to get there.

Every choice God makes, He does it through love. As you pause today, think about how God is your friend and is there to talk to and provide counsel when you need it most.

PRAY

Father God, I lift to you what I am struggling with today. I thank you that your love is never ending and you will hold me in this situation. I pray that you will lead and guide me in the way forward, as I trust in you as a friend. Leaning on your wisdom and understanding. Amen.

MOVE

There are many ways to move across a space. By this I mean moving from point A to point B. For example, you begin at a door as you enter a room and finish at the window on the far side of the room. There are three parts to this Move section today:

1. Explore different ways of travelling across the space.
2. Travel across the space thinking about what you are struggling with currently. How does it change from when you were simply exploring?
3. Invite Jesus to travel the space with you as you move through the struggle you were exploring. Allow Jesus to travel with you.

SONG SUGGESTION

'When You Walk into the Room' by Bryan and Katie Torwalt

MOVE IT FURTHER

From the different ways of travelling you have explored, consider one movement that you feel demonstrates Jesus being your friend. Explore how that movement can be with you consistently as you move across the space. How is this different to when you just invited Jesus?

JOURNAL

How has this verse impacted your dance and movement journey today?
- This happened when I moved…
- Thank you for…
- Please help me with…
- Inspiration came from…

DAY
11

Wait for the LORD;
be strong and take heart
and wait for the LORD.

PSALM 27:14

PAUSE

What do you struggle to wait for? God talks a lot about waiting in the Bible and how important is to **wait** and wait well. Often, we get hung up on waiting being a stationary activity. However, through our waiting we can grow in our understanding of what we are waiting for – learning trust, acceptance and recognising all the other areas that God is moving in. Therefore, waiting is no longer stationary: it's active and requires participation. How can you be more active in your waiting?

PRAY

Father God, I am sorry for the times that I chose not to wait and rushed ahead. Please help me to be strong and firm in my waiting. Thank you for those things which you draw my focus to. These are areas that you are always working in. Help me to continue to see and recognise them. Amen.

MOVE

Think about the following words: 'waiting', 'strength' and 'heart'. What movements depict these words best? What do these words mean to you currently? How can you reflect that in movement, whether stationary or moving?

SONG SUGGESTION

'Awake My Soul' by Hillsong Worship

MOVE IT FURTHER

Put together a series of three to four movements that explore the words 'strength' and 'heart'. Then choose to add in times of waiting between some of the movements.

Subsequently, this becomes a prayer for strength, waiting in that strength – a prayer for the heart and waiting in the heart. This sequence can be repeated several times to allow you to recognise the importance of being active in your waiting.

JOURNAL

How has this verse impacted your dance and movement journey today?

- This happened when I moved...
- Thank you for...
- Please help me with...
- Inspiration came from...

DAY
12

That person is like a tree planted by streams of water,
which yields its fruit in season
and whose leaf does not wither—
whatever they do prospers.

PSALM 1:3

PAUSE

Are you soaking up all that is available to you to help you to grow and flourish? A dry person cannot **hydrate** a dry person. If your spiritual tank is low, take the time to refill it. As you pause today think about how full your spiritual tank is.

What helps to fill it, for it to swell and for you to feel full?

PRAY

Father God, I thank you that we have your word, your church and your people to encourage us to grow and flourish. Please help me with [insert struggle], *to dig deep and hydrate in your strength, recognising when I need a refill and stepping into your presence. Amen.*

MOVE

Imagine you are a tree or flower that is very dry and needs hydrating. Gradually, water and moisture start to seep into the soil until the earth is flooded and it's all there to be soaked up. What does your body want to do in response to this?

SONG SUGGESTION

'Crashing In' by Mezzo Piano

MOVE IT FURTHER

Create two sequences about a personal struggle. The first shows how you are feeling about it now. The second shows what happens when God has hydrated you and you are letting Him help you grow.

If you are struggling to do this, think about how you feel and what your body does when you haven't had enough water to drink. Then, think about the opposite, when you have enough, and what feelings that brings.

JOURNAL

How has this verse impacted your dance and movement journey today?

- This happened when I moved…
- Thank you for…
- Please help me with…
- Inspiration came from…

DAY
13

Whoever dwells in the shelter of the Most High
will rest in the shadow of the Almighty.

PSALM 91:1

PAUSE

God wants to scoop us up and cover us when we need rest. Where has rest featured in your life in the last week? Have you supported yourself in this way?

As you pause today, consider how important **rest** and self-care is to you.

What one thing can you do to look after yourself more?

PRAY

Father God, please help me to recognise the need for rest, both for my own wellbeing and the opportunity it provides to seek moments of quiet to just be. Amen.

MOVE

In a clear, quiet space, close your eyes and take some deep breaths. After you have taken this pause, you discover that God is standing behind you. His purpose as He stands there is to cheer you on with some rest possibilities – activities, emotions, places where you find rest. As you experience this, what movement does your body want to do?

SONG SUGGESTION

'The Shadow of the Almighty' by The Miller Brothers

MOVE IT FURTHER

With your eyes closed, explore raising body parts against a resistance, then dropping them. Then explore lifting and moving them with grace and ease. Which is easier? How can you apply this to seeking rest?

JOURNAL

How has this verse impacted your dance and movement journey today?

- This happened when I moved…
- Thank you for…
- Please help me with…
- Inspiration came from…

DAY
14

Trust in him at all times, you people;
pour out your hearts to him,
for God is our refuge.

PSALM 62:8

PAUSE

Do you chat to God like he's your friend? Do you seek **refuge** in Him?

He loves it when we talk to Him. More of His character is revealed and there is a trust that allows us to go deeper with Him. Pause today and think about what you have discovered about God's character recently.

Have you spoken to Him about what you found out?

PRAY

Father God, help me to pour my heart out to you, to see you as my friend and refuge when things get tough. Help me to trust that you are there for me and see different aspects of your character as I go from day to day. Amen.

MOVE

Thinking about the following words, create some movements to each of these words: 'trust', 'refuge' and 'hearts'. Consider the following things as you explore:

- What stops you trusting God? What helps you to trust God?
- How is God your refuge? How does that make you feel?

SONG SUGGESTION

'Rescue' by Bethel Music, Lauren Daigle

MOVE IT FURTHER

Think about the following phrase: 'Pour out your hearts to him'. As you take that on board personally, how can that be shown with movement?

When I explore phrases such as this, I find that closing my eyes, putting in a pause before I move and choosing to wait can help.

JOURNAL

How has this verse impacted your dance and movement journey today?

- This happened when I moved...
- Thank you for...
- Please help me with...
- Inspiration came from...

PART THREE
Armour of God

Part Three takes us to the Armour of God. It's such a powerful tool but we can forget about its effectiveness for change and the impact it can have on our life. As we enter Part Three, you are encouraged to be more creative as you explore some of these themes. Some of them will run into each other and you may find yourself exploring more verses on one day than on others. Let God lead you.

DAY
15

For our struggle is not against flesh and blood, but against the rulers, against the authorities, against the powers of this dark world and against the spiritual forces of evil in the heavenly realms.

EPHESIANS 6:12

PAUSE

What is currently holding you back?

There can be many things that influence us and the people around us in the world. But God doesn't want us to struggle. As you pause today, choose to voice out loud what is holding you back from moving forward.

PRAY

Father God, I thank you that you are above all of our struggles, you lead the way and you guide. Please instil in me a knowledge that you carry me through my struggles. Thank you for all the struggles you have already helped me through. Amen.

MOVE

Pick something that you are struggling with at the moment. Pause and then create three movements that depict your struggle. Then, take another pause and focus on where you can see God supporting you through the struggle. Create another three movements for what this means to you.

SONG SUGGESTION

'Every Giant Will Fall' by Rend Collective

MOVE IT FURTHER

Taking your two sets of three movements, join them together. This can be done by adding some travelling in between. Then, as you complete the sequence, you will be transitioning from what things were to what things will be.

JOURNAL

How has this verse impacted your dance and movement journey today?

- This happened when I moved…
- Thank you for…
- Please help me with…
- Inspiration came from…

DAY
16

Therefore, put on the full armor of God, so that when the day of evil comes, you may be able to stand your ground, and after you have done everything, to stand.

EPHESIANS 6:13

PAUSE

How strong is your anchor in God? We can't be prepared for what is to come if we've made no effort to be ready. God has all the equipment waiting; we just need to step out and use it.

As you pause today, write down how many times you have put on the 'armor of God' and the result it has brought as you did it.

PRAY

Father God, please help me to use you as my anchor. Help me to connect and stand my ground when things get tough, knowing that you have equipped me with what I need. Thank you that we have this armour which we can wear to help us live our lives daily. Amen.

MOVE

Imagine something sticky is on your feet. How can you move from where you are? What helps you move better? Explore this for a couple of minutes. Now imagine that God is that stickiness. How does that change how you move? What do you need to move through the stickiness with ease?

SONG SUGGESTION

'Let Everything (Praise the Lord)' by Pat Barrett

MOVE IT FURTHER

Read 1 Corinthians 15:58 and Colossians 2:6–7. Do your movements change when you relate what you are doing directly to these verses?

JOURNAL

How has this verse impacted your dance and movement journey today?

- This happened when I moved…
- Thank you for…
- Please help me with…
- Inspiration came from…

DAY
17

Stand firm then, with the belt of truth buckled round your waist, with the breastplate of righteousness in place...

EPHESIANS 6:14

PAUSE

Where in your life do you need to speak or hear more truth? God's truths are everywhere in the Bible. But do we acknowledge the ones that will help us the most or the ones that we need to hear more?

As you pause today, recognise where you need more of God's truth and how you can demonstrate more of His truth in your everyday.

PRAY

Father God, you are the one that speaks truth into my life. You are the one who enables me to act righteously in instances when it might normally be hard. Help me to keep hearing and receiving those truths that you have for me. Thank you for the way I can demonstrate your truth already. Amen.

MOVE

Identify some truths from the following Scriptures:

For the Spirit God gave us does not make us timid, but gives us power, love and self-discipline. 2 TIMOTHY 1:7

Therefore, if anyone is in Christ, the new creation has come. The old has gone, the new is here! 2 CORINTHIANS 5:17

I praise you because I am fearfully and wonderfully made; your works are wonderful, I know that full well. PSALM 139:14

Once you have identified the truths, put them to movement as a way of accepting what God has said to you.

SONG SUGGESTION

'Another in the Fire' by Hillsong UNITED

MOVE IT FURTHER

Combine three to four of the truths that you identified in the Scriptures above into a sequence. Then think about what wearing a belt does (holds in, supports core, helps posture) and incorporate these movements into the sequence.

JOURNAL

How has this verse impacted your dance and movement journey today?

- This happened when I moved...
- Thank you for...
- Please help me with...
- Inspiration came from...

DAY
18

*... and with your feet fitted with the readiness
that comes from the gospel of peace.*

EPHESIANS 6:15

PAUSE

How do you or could you share God's word? Part of being a Christian is the desire to share with others the love God has for us, to draw people in and share our excitement.

Pause today and remember when you last shared God's word. Were you excited?

PRAY

Father God, help me to feel excitement over fear about sharing your word. Help me to see I am enough just as I am. Bring me a sense of peace and help me to lean into you as I do this. Amen.

MOVE

Today's movement involves exploring leaning on someone. To begin with though, find a wall or something sturdy to lean against. What does it feel like to lean on the wall? How does it support you? What does your body do? Now imagine you are leaning against God. Does that change what you are feeling or experiencing at all?

SONG SUGGESTION

'Jericho Song' by Rend Co. Kids

MOVE IT FURTHER

The Holy Spirit helps us to share God's word. How does the Holy Spirit move through our bodies? Can that impact the way we move when we know we're leaning on God?

JOURNAL

How has this verse impacted your dance and movement journey today?

- This happened when I moved…
- Thank you for…
- Please help me with…
- Inspiration came from…

DAY
19

In addition to all this, take up the shield of faith, with which you can extinguish all the flaming arrows of the evil one.

EPHESIANS 6:16

PAUSE

How strong is your shield? What arrows are you fighting against? God's shield gives us refuge, protection and strength with the help of the Holy Spirit.

Pause today and make a note of how strong your shield is, as well as the arrows that you feel you are fighting against.

PRAY

Father God, only by standing in faith can we extinguish the flaming arrows. Help me to be strong and secure knowing that you will divert and break any arrows coming my way. Thank you for the arrows that you have already diverted and shielded me from. Amen.

MOVE

How do you react if something is coming at you and you want to deflect it? There is both a 'reaction' and 'action' in responding to something coming at you. This 'something' could be a physical or emotional thing. Thinking about this, explore different ways movement could demonstrate the opposites that these words are implying. Don't forget about levels and using big and small movements.

SONG SUGGESTION

'The Best is Yet to Come' by Patrick Mayberry

MOVE IT FURTHER

Think about how a normal arrow moves and then how a flaming arrow moves. Create a movement for each. How do they differ? Do the movements you created before about reacting to something coming towards you change based on this arrow exploration?

JOURNAL

How has this verse impacted your dance and movement journey today?

- This happened when I moved...
- Thank you for...
- Please help me with...
- Inspiration came from...

DAY
20

*Take the helmet of salvation and the
sword of the Spirit, which is the word of God.*

EPHESIANS 6:17

PAUSE

How does God's word sustain us? The word of God is living and active; the 'helmet of Salvation' protects our head. Our head contains our focus, emotions and clarity. The sword of the Spirit protects our ability to stand on God's word.

Pause today, thinking about how God's word sustains you, where your focus is and how strong you feel able to stand on God's word.

PRAY

Father God, I thank you that your word keeps us going. I thank you that we can learn and grow as we read more about you. Please help me to turn to you for clarity and focus when needed. I thank you that you help give us a clear head. Amen.

MOVE

Identify someone that you are praying for currently. Ask God to lead and guide you in a movement prayer for them. Think of a Scripture that may help sustain them and offer clarity, which they may need, providing support for their emotions and input from the Holy Spirit to guide and help them feel well.

SONG SUGGESTION

'Through All of It' by Colton Dixon

MOVE IT FURTHER

Take the movement prayer that you have created and share it with the person you were praying for. If you are able to record it and send it, do that. If you can't, just let them know that you moved out a prayer for them today.

JOURNAL

How has this verse impacted your dance and movement journey today?

- This happened when I moved…
- Thank you for…
- Please help me with…
- Inspiration came from…

DAY
21

And pray in the Spirit on all occasions with all kinds of prayers and requests. With this in mind, be alert and always keep on praying for all the Lord's people.

EPHESIANS 6:18

PAUSE

Where do you need to focus your prayer so that any limits can be lifted? God encourages us to always be praying, to always be alert, seeking and supporting – noticing!

Pause today and consider how your prayer life could be more focused.

PRAY

Father God, you know the dreams that are inside me and where my life will go. Please protect me as I step out and trust where you will lead me and help me to notice the small things. Thank you for helping me to focus my prayers when needed. Please help me to continue to do this. Amen.

MOVE

Play the suggested song below. Reflect on the lyrics and spend a moment recognising that God gives you peace. Then move out what peace feels to you.

SONG SUGGESTION

'Peace Be Still' by Lauren Daigle

MOVE IT FURTHER

Create a small sequence that can become your 'peace sequence' – a series of moves for when you need to pray but don't know how you can move. God knows!

JOURNAL

How has this verse impacted your dance and movement journey today?

- This happened when I moved…
- Thank you for…
- Please help me with…
- Inspiration came from…

PART FOUR

God's Truths

Part Four is exciting. There are so many points in the Bible where God's truths are spoken. You are encouraged to explore pictures or static positions through your movements, adding in travel, as well as allowing moments of stillness. God's truths are there to uplift and carry us when we struggle. Choose to dig deep and accept what you discover in this section.

DAY
22

*Have I not commanded you? Be strong
and courageous. Do not be afraid; do not be
discouraged, for the LORD your God will be with
you wherever you go."*

JOSHUA 1:9

PAUSE

God is right there with you when you feel in the pit of despair; He wants
to carry you and uphold you. He will give you all the **strength** that you
need to do that.

Pause today and tell God you are not afraid. Choose to recognise that
God is with you wherever you go.

PRAY

*Father God, I pray for strength to carry out what I need to do. Help me to
stand strong, trust you and have courage. Amen*

MOVE

Pick three adjectives from today's verse and create a static position for each. Think how they impact you and what they mean to you. Go through each of the movements, choosing to have a slight pause between each one. This will allow you to put actions to the words, helping you to remember their significance.

SONG SUGGESTION

'Everlasting God' by Chris Tomlin

MOVE IT FURTHER

How can this Scripture impact your life? Take time to create a series of movements that could show a picture of movements demonstrating this. Join it to the sequence that you created earlier.

JOURNAL

How has this verse impacted your dance and movement journey today?

- This happened when I moved…
- Thank you for…
- Please help me with…
- Inspiration came from…

DAY
23

And he who searches our hearts knows the mind of the Spirit, because the Spirit intercedes for God's people in accordance with the will of God.

ROMANS 8:27

PAUSE

The Holy Spirit helps us to **intercede** for others: you step into the gap when no one else can.

Pause today and think about how you can step into the gap (you can read Ezekiel 22:30 for more understanding on this) for someone else today – a friend or family member who you know might be struggling.

PRAY

Father God, help me to step into the gap for someone today, bringing them closer to you and encouraging them on their journey with you. Amen.

MOVE

Ask God for someone that you can step into the gap and pray for. Think about how the Spirit moves and create three or four movements as a prayer for that person. Choose to demonstrate how the Spirit can come alongside those who are struggling and support them.

SONG SUGGESTION

'Standing in Miracles' (Instrumental) by Lighthouse Piano

MOVE IT FURTHER

Spend some time asking God for a specific word for that person. Step that out into a movement prayer and share it with them if you feel that's an appropriate thing to do.

JOURNAL

How has this verse impacted your dance and movement journey today?

- This happened when I moved…
- Thank you for…
- Please help me with…
- Inspiration came from…

DAY
24

Dear children, let us not love with words or speech but with actions and in truth. This is how we know that we belong to the truth and how we set our hearts at rest in his presence:

1 JOHN 3:18-19

PAUSE

The **truth** that we share about God should consume us in our everyday and how we lead our lives. Are you sharing God's truth in your actions?

As you pause today, think about how you have acted over the past week and whether it has demonstrated God's character.

PRAY

Father God, I thank you that we have your truths in the Bible to live by. Please help us to be active in living them out and demonstrating what they are. Thank you for the opportunities that you give us to do this. Amen.

MOVE

Which word or words stand out from today's verses? How would you respond in movement? Begin by exploring the first thing that comes to mind and then growing and expanding that thought or feeling.

SONG SUGGESTION

'Know You' (feat. Steffany Gretzinger) by Koryn Hawthorne

MOVE IT FURTHER

Connect the movements that you have identified above together and explore what it feels like to know that 'we belong to the truth'.

JOURNAL

How have these verses impacted your dance and movement journey today?

- This happened when I moved…
- Thank you for…
- Please help me with…
- Inspiration came from…

DAY
25

Each of you should use whatever gift you have received to serve others, as faithful stewards of God's grace in its various forms.

I PETER 4:10

PAUSE

Do you recognise the gifts that God has given you? His desire is that you overflow in them as you **serve** and, as you overflow, others notice and want to know more.

Pause today and think about how you serve. How do you use your gifts for others?

PRAY

Father God, thank you for the gifts you have given me. I am sorry for those times I haven't stepped out and served with them. Please help me to lean on you to do this more. Amen.

MOVE

Think about one of the gifts that God has given you. How does that equip you to serve others sharing God's word? Stand still with your hands open, palms up. Ask God's spirit to fill up inside you from your toes through to your head. As the Holy Spirit comes, begin to move out the gift you have identified, lifting it up with thankfulness to God.

SONG SUGGESTION

'Heavenly' by Pat Barrett

MOVE IT FURTHER

Continue to take some time to think about the other gifts God has given you. Close your eyes and choose to receive each one of them from God. As you receive them, begin to say thank you in movement.

JOURNAL

How has this verse impacted your dance and movement journey today?

- This happened when I moved…
- Thank you for…
- Please help me with…
- Inspiration came from…

DAY
26

If anyone speaks, they should do so as one who speaks the very words of God. If anyone serves, they should do so with the strength God provides, so that in all things God may be praised through Jesus Christ. To him be the glory and the power for ever and ever. Amen.

I PETER 4:11

PAUSE

Serving others can require strength you didn't know you had; this strength comes from God. In those moments, His provision prevails, and He guides you to speak and **serve** as needed. Pause today and consider the inner strength that you have.

How has that served you and helped you in the times when you needed it most?

PRAY

Father God, I thank you that I can speak and demonstrate your word through serving. I thank you for providing me with strength for those times when it's hardest. Please help me to continue to praise you through my serving. Amen.

MOVE

Using the words 'strength' and 'praise', create a freeze or a movement for each word to demonstrate what those words mean to you with God at the helm. Cycle through the two movements several times, taking each one on board.

SONG SUGGESTION

'Praise Your Name' by Corey Voss, Madison Street Worship

MOVE IT FURTHER

Expand the movements you created above in the following ways:

- Do one variation that remains still with minimum effort.
- Create a second variation with energy, bounce and excitement.
- How different do the two sequences feel?

JOURNAL

How has this verse impacted your dance and movement journey today?

- This happened when I moved…
- Thank you for…
- Please help me with…
- Inspiration came from…

DAY
27

Be joyful in hope, patient in affliction,
faithful in prayer.

ROMANS 12:12

PAUSE

God understands that there are days when to sit and **pray** is hard, when words can't come and just emotions sit there. But God hears your thoughts, feels your pain and knows your faith.

As you pause today, think about the moments in life currently where you want to feel joy but are struggling with pain.

Allow God to seep into parts of that situation to bring joy to it.

PRAY

Father God, I thank you that, through it all, I can praise you and pray to you. When words don't come, you take my emotions, my movements, my song and receive them as a prayer. I thank you that I have the ability to do this. Amen.

MOVE

Create movements for the whole verse to make a prayer to use when things are hard, and words don't come easily. This is best done by segmenting the verse into small chunks and focusing on a little bit at a time. Think about what the words mean to you and how they impact your walk with God.

SONG SUGGESTION

'Joy Pours Out' (Instrumental) by Christy Nockels

MOVE IT FURTHER

Think about one thing you are praying for now. Create some movements and add that into the sequence you created for the verse.

JOURNAL

How has this verse impacted your dance and movement journey today?

- This happened when I moved…
- Thank you for…
- Please help me with…
- Inspiration came from…

DAY
28

This is what the LORD says:

"Stand at the crossroads and look; ask for the ancient paths, ask where the good way is, and walk in it, and you will find rest for your souls. But you said, 'We will not walk in it.'"

JEREMIAH 6:16

PAUSE

Saying to God we won't walk the path He puts before us makes Him sad. But, equally, He knows the pathways that you are going to take before you step into them. His heart wants to lead you on the right **pathways**. Your heart needs to be open to look and hear where those pathways are. Today, pause and think about when you might have said no to God for a pathway he's put before you. Then consider how God has still been there on that pathway anyway.

PRAY

Father God, I am sorry for those times I don't look and I choose another path. Please help me to pause and seek the way that you want me to go. Thank you for how you are with me regardless of what path I take. Please help me recognise how you are with me on the pathways where I struggle. Amen.

MOVE

Explore ways that you travel. Think about…

- Forwards, backwards, side to side.
- What happens when something gets in your way?
- How do you react? Where do your movements go?
- How does God lead and guide you on different pathways?

SONG SUGGESTION

'I Choose to Worship' by Rend Collective

MOVE IT FURTHER

Think about your journey over the past month. Draw what you think that looks like. Transfer the image you have created on paper to movement. What does it feel like? Can you see the movements God was with you the most in?

JOURNAL

How has this verse impacted your dance and movement journey today?

- This happened when I moved…
- Thank you for…
- Please help me with…
- Inspiration came from…

DAY
29

Let us then approach God's throne of grace with confidence, so that we may receive mercy and find grace to help us in our time of need.

HEBREWS 4:16

PAUSE

What does the word **mercy** mean to you? God's mercy is beyond what we can imagine, full of love, compassion and patience that overflows in unexpected and unmerited ways.

Take a moment today and think how God's mercy, love and compassion has woven into your life.

PRAY

Father God, I thank you that you give us the confidence to receive your mercy and find your grace. Please help me to rest in that confidence and know that you are always there in my time of need. Amen.

MOVE

Stand in the room you are in – or head outside! Choose a point away from you. If you're outside, try and make it at least 10 metres away. That place, set away from you, is God's throne of grace. How will you approach it?

SONG SUGGESTION

'Throne of Grace' by Highlands Worship

MOVE IT FURTHER

What do you need more confidence with? Create a movement that depicts this and use it to approach God's throne of grace. Is the movement any different to how you did it before?

JOURNAL

How has this verse impacted your dance and movement journey today?

- This happened when I moved…
- Thank you for…
- Please help me with…
- Inspiration came from…

DAY
30

*but those who hope in the LORD will renew their strength.
They will soar on wings like eagles; they will run and not
grow weary, they will walk and not be faint.*

ISAIAH 40:31

PAUSE

When we let God into situations, He can support us, carry us and give
us strength. How often do we try to do things without letting God do
those things for us?

Pause today and think about where you'd like God to **renew** your
strength and how you would like to soar, knowing that God was lifting
you through that situation.

PRAY

*Father God, I thank you that you pick us up during those times when we
are struggling, and you support us moving forward. Please help me to
rest in your embrace and put my hope in you during those times. Thank
you for those times I feel I am soaring and the joy it brings. Help me to
remember them when I am struggling. Amen.*

MOVE

Think about the word 'soar'. What movements does it invoke and what feelings does it bring? If someone soars with you, does it change things?

SONG SUGGESTION

'What a Beautiful Name' by The Maker & The Instrument

MOVE IT FURTHER

Break down the verse and create movements to the following things:

- Hope
- What you need renewed strength for
- Soaring
- Weariness
- Walk

Join some of these movements with what you explored above.

JOURNAL

How has this verse impacted your dance and movement journey today?

- This happened when I moved...
- Thank you for...
- Please help me with...
- Inspiration came from...

DAY
31

For where your treasure is, there your
heart will be also.

LUKE 12:34

PAUSE

What do you treasure in your life? God's **treasure** is greater than anything else, He wants us to seek it, hold it, love it and want more of it.

Pause today and think about how you can make sure you treasure the right things.

PRAY

Father God, help me to treasure what you have given me and how you love me. I am sorry for the times this is not central in my heart. Please open my eyes when those moments occur and help me to rejoice in all that you have given me. Amen

MOVE

Using a piece of material or a scarf as an aid, explore hiding, revealing and discovering it. Think about how the material flows and what it does as you move. God's heart is for us to discover His treasure, so consider this as you move too.

SONG SUGGESTION

'When I Say Jesus' (Live) by Life.Church Worship

MOVE IT FURTHER

Think of one treasure God has given you (faith, patience, movement, love, joy etc). Using a piece of material or a scarf as an aid , explore hiding, revealing and discovering it.

JOURNAL

How has this verse impacted your dance and movement journey today?

- This happened when I moved...
- Thank you for...
- Please help me with...
- Inspiration came from...

DAY
32

*Humble yourselves, therefore, under
God's mighty hand, that he may lift you
up in due time.*

I PETER 5:6

PAUSE

As we have free will, emotions, thoughts and actions, this sometimes means that we don't always react or act the right way in situations and relationships.

But God's word calls us to be humble and bow before Him. As you pause today, recognise where you need to be **humble** and bow before God. Choose to allow Him to lead the situation.

PRAY

Father God, please help me to be humble in those situations when I want to stand up and be different. Teach me to lean into your word and walk humbly. Thank you for how you move as we bow before you. Amen.

MOVE

Take a moment and imagine God's mighty hand is over you right now. How do you respond to this? In what way do you want to move? Do you feel acceptance, excitement, comfort, joy, peace, humbleness? Or something else?

SONG SUGGESTION

'Anything is Possible' (Live) by Bethel Music, Dante Bowe

MOVE IT FURTHER

What words do you feel when you know that God's mighty hand is over you? Create a movement for each of these words. Repeat the movements several times and use a prayer of thanks, lifting them up to God.

JOURNAL

How has this verse impacted your dance and movement journey today?

- This happened when I moved…
- Thank you for…
- Please help me with…
- Inspiration came from…

DAY
33

They replied, "The Lord needs it." They brought it to Jesus, threw their cloaks on the colt and put Jesus on it. As he went along, people spread their cloaks on the road. When he came near the place where the road goes down the Mount of Olives, the whole crowd of disciples began joyfully to praise God in loud voices for all the miracles they had seen: "Blessed is the king who comes in the name of the Lord!" "Peace in heaven and glory in the highest!"

LUKE 19:34–38

PAUSE

Is **praising** God part of your everyday? The crowds here prepared the way for Jesus to come and joyfully declare all that God has done. Pause today and look back on your week. What can you praise God for? Going forward, choose to write one thing down every day that praises God.

PRAY

Father God, I thank you that you prepare the way before us. I pray that I can praise you throughout my day, preparing the way for others to follow their path to you. Thank you for the days I've chosen to praise even when I've struggled. Amen.

MOVE

Begin by developing this phrase: 'joyfully to praise God' into movement. Then pick two to three words from the rest of the verse to add to the sequence using movement. These could be words that speak to you or ones that you feel link in well with the phrase above.

SONG SUGGESTION

'Raise a Hallelujah' (Studio Version) by Bethel Music, Jonathan David Hesler, Melissa Hesler

MOVE IT FURTHER

Being joyful and praising in our everyday involves doing it through all emotions. Think about three levels – low, medium and high – and develop the sequence you created earlier based on these three levels. This could be done in terms of three emotions that you feel about praising God sometimes.

JOURNAL

How have these verses impacted your dance and movement journey today?

- This happened when I moved…
- Thank you for…
- Please help me with…
- Inspiration came from…

DAY
34

As Jesus looked up, he saw the rich putting their gifts into the temple treasury. He also saw a poor widow put in two very small copper coins. "Truly I tell you," he said, "this poor widow has put in more than all the others. All these people gave their gifts out of their wealth; but she out of her poverty put in all she had to live on."

LUKE 21:1–4

PAUSE

As you pause today, think about what you have done this week that cost you something – physically, emotionally, monetarily? God calls us to gives ourselves as a living sacrifice. Sometimes that means **offering** something when there is nothing. God values this and sees your heart through it. How can you be more intentional about this?

PRAY

Father God, encourage me in those moments when I think I have nothing to give and offer. Help me to realise that my offering, no matter how big or small, has value. Amen.

MOVE

Make up some moves to demonstrate bringing an offering to someone. You can also explore bringing an offering before God. What does that look like for you?

SONG SUGGESTION

'Lead Me to the Cross' (Instrumental) by Mezzo Piano

MOVE IT FURTHER

Think of one thing that you could bring as an offering (or gift). Ask God to lead you as you transpose that into a prayer. You could link the movements that you create in with what you explored earlier.

JOURNAL

How have these verses impacted your dance and movement journey today?

- This happened when I moved…
- Thank you for…
- Please help me with…
- Inspiration came from…

PART FIVE
The Journey of the Cross

As Part Five gets under way, we begin by looking at the journey Jesus took to the cross. Who He met on the way and how that impacts our lives. Jesus did so much for us, but the reality of acknowledging, receiving and putting into practice His word and His journey can be much harder.

DAY
35

*And he took bread, gave thanks and broke it,
and gave it to them, saying, "This is my body
given for you; do this in remembrance of me."*

*In the same way, after the supper he took the
cup, saying, "This cup is the new covenant in my
blood, which is poured out for you.*

LUKE 22:19–20

PAUSE

Jesus gave us a way to acknowledge the **communion** we have between
Him and ourselves.

How often do you take a pause to remember that His body was broken
and His blood was poured out for you?

PRAY

*Father God, I thank you that you gave your body and blood for us. I am
sorry for the times I haven't acknowledged this and lost my way from the
communion between myself and you. Please help me to remember. Amen.*

MOVE

Pick out three words from today's verses and create movements to them. Place a pause between each movement as an acknowledgement to remember what Jesus did.

SONG SUGGESTION

'Table of the Lord' by Soul Survivor, Tom Smith

MOVE IT FURTHER

Look at the verses. What feelings do they invoke inside you? Write them down. Create a short sequence for the verses, then adapt the sequence with two of the feelings you identified.

JOURNAL

How have these verses impacted your dance and movement journey today?

- This happened when I moved…
- Thank you for…
- Please help me with…
- Inspiration came from…

DAY
36

*... "Pray that you will not fall into temptation."
He withdrew ... prayed, "Father, if you are
willing, take this cup from me; yet not my
will, but yours be done." An angel from heaven
appeared to him and strengthened him. ... he
prayed more earnestly ...*

LUKE 22:39–44
[excerpt above, read section in full]

PAUSE

As you pause today, think about when you pray and the conversations
you have with God. Where do you feel most at home with **prayer**? For
what issue do you need to say to God, 'not my will but yours'? What do
you need more strength with through prayer? Acknowledge this and lift
it up to God.

PRAY

*Father God, I thank you that we can look to you for strength and pray
when we realise that we are being tempted. Lead me on the right path to
say, 'your will not mine'. Amen.*

MOVE

Think about the questions posed in the Pause section. How would you answer them? Put these questions to movement.

SONG SUGGESTION

'Gethsemene' by Andy and Wendy Green

MOVE IT FURTHER

Think about different levels – high, medium and low – and how integrating your movements can change the dynamics. Apply this to the movements that you explored above. How do the changes in levels and dynamics help you understand your prayer journey more?

JOURNAL

How have these verses impacted your dance and movement journey today?

- This happened when I moved…
- Thank you for…
- Please help me with…
- Inspiration came from…

DAY
37

As the soldiers led him away, they seized Simon from Cyrene, who was on his way in from the country, and put the cross on him and made him carry it behind Jesus … Jesus said, "Father, forgive them, for they do not know what they are doing." … There was a written notice above him, which read: THIS IS THE KING OF THE JEWS. … Jesus answered him, "Truly I tell you, today you will be with me in paradise."

LUKE 23:26–43
[excerpt above, read section in full]

PAUSE

As you pause today, consider the answers to the following questions. How heavy would the cross be? What would your body do in response to having to carry something heavy? What things do you need to ask **forgiveness** for? How would you feel if you were accused of being something you weren't?

PRAY

Father God, please help me to identify anything I need to ask forgiveness for. I thank you that your Son carried the cross and stepped into the gap for us. Help me recognise the strength you have given me, both inside and outside, to live life well through your Son's death. Amen.

MOVE

Explore what it might be like to carry something heavy, as well as what you might need to ask forgiveness for. Build together a series of movements for this.

SONG SUGGESTION

'Anchor of Peace' by North Point Worship, Desi Raines

MOVE IT FURTHER

Identify one thing that you need forgiveness for or someone/thing that you need to forgive. Beginning low down, imagine receiving that forgiveness and growing tall and strong, knowing God's got you. How do your movements develop?

JOURNAL

How have these verses impacted your dance and movement journey today?

- This happened when I moved...
- Thank you for...
- Please help me with...
- Inspiration came from...

DAY
38

It was now about noon, and darkness came over the whole land until three in the afternoon, for the sun stopped shining. And the curtain of the temple was torn in two. Jesus called out with a loud voice, "Father, into your hands I commit my spirit." When he had said this, he breathed his last.

LUKE 23:44-46

PAUSE

How can you show **light** in darkness? What do you need to commit to the Lord?

Pause today and think about how you can add **breath** into the situation? Grab some pens and draw some pictures demonstrating light and dark and what they mean to you.

PRAY

Father God, I thank you that your light shines bright through all situations. I thank you that, through your death, you bring us hope. Please help me to shine bright for you. Amen.

MOVE

Explore movements that would represent darkness and then movements that represent light. Transition between light and darkness movements, asking God to bring light into more of your darkness.

SONG SUGGESTION

'No Longer I' (Live) by Elim Sound

MOVE IT FURTHER

Consider your daily routine. Where can you add more breath? How can you do that? What does it feel like to add more pauses between movements?

JOURNAL

How have theses verses impacted your dance and movement journey today?

- This happened when I moved...
- Thank you for...
- Please help me with...
- Inspiration came from...

DAY
39

Now there was a man named Joseph ... Going to Pilate, he asked for Jesus' body. Then he took it down, wrapped it in linen cloth and placed it in a tomb cut in the rock, one in which no one had yet been laid ... But they rested on the Sabbath in obedience to the commandment.

LUKE 23:50–56
[excerpt above, read section in full]

PAUSE

Pause today and remember the **precious gift** that God gave you. How does it feel moving and holding something precious? Are there scenarios when it's easier to move that precious thing?

Where do you implement rest in your life currently? How could you add more rest in?

PRAY

Father God, thank you for the precious things that you give me. Help me to identify the moments in my life where I need to see a pause, a breath, a moment of peace. Amen.

MOVE

How precious to you is it that Jesus died for you? Spend some time reflecting on what Jesus did for you. What does that look like in movement? Also consider your answers to the other questions posed in the Pause section.

SONG SUGGESTION

'The Father's House' by Mezzo Piano

MOVE IT FURTHER

Find a place outside that you find restful. Identify some of the movements that you put together above. Consider adding different levels and rest into the movements and find peace in God's creation.

JOURNAL

How have these verses impacted your dance and movement journey today?

- This happened when I moved…
- Thank you for…
- Please help me with…
- Inspiration came from…

DAY
40

On the first day of the week, very early in the morning, the women took the spices they had prepared and went to the tomb. They found the stone rolled away from the tomb, but when they entered, they did not find the body of the Lord Jesus. While they were wondering about this, suddenly two men in clothes that gleamed like lightning stood beside them. In their fright the women bowed down with their faces to the ground, but the men said to them, "Why do you look for the living among the dead? He is not here; he has risen! Remember how he told you, while he was still with you in Galilee: 'The Son of Man must be delivered over to the hands of sinners, be crucified and on the third day be raised again.'" Then they remembered his words.

LUKE 24:1–8

PAUSE

What's your response when you can't find something that's precious? How excited would you be when you found it again? As you pause today, write down five things that bring you **JOY** right now.

PRAY

Father God, I thank you that we have so much to be thankful for. I thank you that there is always joy in life. Please help me to find joy in those times when I find it hardest. Amen.

MOVE

Take your five things of joy and add one to two movements to each of the things. Think about why they bring you joy and whether that changes your movement.

SONG SUGGESTION

'Love Changes Everything' (Live) by Red Rocks Worship

'Child of Love' (Live) by We The Kingdom

'Might Get Loud' by Elevation Worship, Chris Brown, Brandon Lake, Tiffany Hudson

MOVE IT FURTHER

Link all your joy movements into one sequence. This is your joy dance. In those moments when you need to remember you are not only precious but that God is with you no matter what, dance your JOY DANCE.

JOURNAL

How have these verses impacted your dance and movement journey today?

- This happened when I moved…
- Thank you for…
- Please help me with…
- Inspiration came from…

CLOSING REFLECTIONS

I hope the journey you have gone on during these devotionals has been transformative and allowed you to realise that God's word surrounds you every day and that God is beside you, cheering you on no matter WHAT the circumstances.

Most of all, I hope that the dance and movement you have experienced in this book has enabled you to create a deeper conversation with God.

I pray this is just the beginning of your journey of exploring God's word in a different way.

May you be blessed as you move forward, with confidence and joy, as you shine bright for Jesus.

MOVING FORWARD

Think about what you have enjoyed the most over the past 40 days. The Scriptures and movements that have caused a change in you and created a lasting impact on your journey. Reflect back on your journal entries and see the way that God moved.

To round off the book, I will share with you some tips to help you continue to explore the Bible and create movement from it.

Each time you are presented with some Scripture, you can run through the following questions yourself to explore the depth it has.

Have confidence in yourself that you can do it. You've just done it for 40 days. Allow the Bible to be a playground, full of fun, exploration and new experiences. Share with others what you discover and invite them to explore it with you!

I'm going to work through the questions with an example so you can see how I would think as I look and analyse a Scripture.

Let's begin by reading Isaiah 42:3

A bruised reed he will not break, and a smoldering wick he will not snuff out. In faithfulness he will bring forth justice;

Firstly ask yourself, "What stands out?"

Look at the Scripture and see which words you are drawn towards. Think about feelings, emotions, settings, history and the spoken word.

As I look at this, I am drawn to the following words and phrases: 'bruised reed', 'break', 'smoldering', 'faithfulness' and 'justice'.

They all echo something that is connected to my journey of faith and how I am feeling as I look at the Scripture.

- No matter how bruised we are, God can always use us and will always support us so we do not break.

- A smouldering wick is something that can't be put out, that keeps going no matter what.

- Following Christ is all about faith – faith in knowing that God has got us and faithfulness to follow the unseen and allow God space to work.

- As we have that faith, God fights for us and brings justice into our journey.

Then, "What movement does the verse show?"

'Movement' can be seen in many different ways. There is the physical way as well as the descriptive way. Study the Scripture and see what movement naturally flows through it.

For me, the Scripture gives me strength, something that glows and keeps going. I would use this as my basis to grow and develop movement.

Then, "How does it make you feel?"

Our reactions to words can change on a daily basis depending on the mindset we have and how we are feeling. The words in this Scripture bring me encouragement, knowing that, whatever I do, God will keep me going.

I have a picture in my mind of pushing through, thinking about the embers that glow.

From there you can convert your thoughts to movement.

All of these thoughts converge into movement. Beginning by looking at my answers to the questions above, I consider height, size, strength, speed and more and how this can change the effect and grow the movement that I have created.

Keep exploring God's word.

Let it grow in your heart and have fun whilst you do it!

SCRIPTURE LIST

These Scriptures are listed in order that they're explored in the book. If they have a supporting word in bold, it is listed beside it.

SONG SUGGESTIONS

These are all songs suggested for use alongside movement. If you gather them up into one playlist, they are then there for you to use when you need to. You can find a YouTube playlist here https://youtube.com/playlist?list=PLE7H1f9JpnUUXi8qWnWzccbkBgHnqL5FG.

Day	Song Suggestion
1.	'Burn Like a Star' by Rend Collective
2.	'Only Jesus' (Instrumental) by Bethel Music
3.	'I See You' by Chris Tomlin, Brandon Lake
4.	'Touch the Sky' by Instrumental Worship Project from I'm In Records
5.	'Be Still' by Hillsong Worship
6.	'Peace Over You' by Here Be Lions
7.	'Don't Hide' (feat. Feranmi Oguns) by Lucy Grimble
8.	'Champion' (Instrumental) by Worship Portal
9.	'Always Good' (Instrumental) by Lighthouse Piano
10.	'When You Walk into the Room' by Bryan and Katie Torwalt
11.	'Awake My Soul' by Hillsong Worship
12.	'Crashing In' by Mezzo Piano
13.	'The Shadow of the Almighty' by The Miller Brothers
14.	'Rescue' by Bethel Music, Lauren Daigle
15.	'Every Giant Will Fall' by Rend Collective
16.	'Let Everything (Praise the Lord)' by Pat Barrett
17.	'Another in the Fire' by Hillsong UNITED
18.	'Jericho Song' by Rend Co. Kids
19.	'The Best is Yet to Come' by Patrick Mayberry
20.	'Through All of It' by Colton Dixon
21.	'Peace Be Still' by Lauren Daigle

22. 'Everlasting God' by Chris Tomlin
23. 'Standing in Miracles' (Instrumental) by Lighthouse Piano
24. 'Know You' (feat. Steffany Gretzinger) by Koryn Hawthorne
25. 'Heavenly' by Pat Barrett
26. 'Praise Your Name' by Corey Voss, Madison Street Worship
27. 'Joy Pours Out' (Instrumental) by Christy Nockels
28. 'I Choose to Worship' by Rend Collective
29. 'Throne of Grace' by Highlands Worship
30. 'What a Beautiful Name' by The Maker & The Instrument
31. 'When I Say Jesus' (Live) by Life.Church Worship
32. 'Anything is Possible' (Live) by Bethel Music, Dante Bowe
33. 'Raise a Hallelujah' (Studio Version) by Bethel Music, Jonathan David Hesler, Melissa Hesler
34. 'Lead Me to the Cross' (Instrumental) by Mezzo Piano
35. 'Table of the Lord' by Soul Survivor, Tom Smith
36. 'Gethsemene' by Andy and Wendy Green
37. 'Anchor of Peace' by North Point Worship, Desi Raines
38. 'No Longer I' (Live) by Elim Sound
39. 'The Father's House' by Mezzo Piano
40. 'Love Changes Everything' (Live) by Red Rocks Worship
    'Child of Love' (Live) by We The Kingdom
    'Might Get Loud' by Elevation Worship, Chris Brown, Brandon Lake, Tiffany Hudson

GLOSSARY OF TERMS

Levels

There are three main ways you can explore levels through movement: low, medium and high. Low may involve a chair or the floor. Medium height tends to be around your waist and your natural standing stance, whilst high is above your head.

This doesn't mean your movement just has to be above your head. Your focus, eyeline and body position can also point in this direction.

Freezes

This is the simplest and primary way to begin creating any type of movement. Think about depicting a picture, something that is frozen, and hold it still.

Travelling

This involves moving from point A to point B in some form. Remember that travelling is not just walking; it can involve many other ways. Here are just a few examples: hop, skip, slide, turn, run, walk, leap, gallop, lunge/stretch.

Transition

This involves moving from one movement to another. Very rarely do we just do one movement and then the next. It can appear very stilted.

Often, we need to think about how we get from one to the other. For example, if you are in a position on the floor and the next position is standing up, you don't simply stand up.

Explore how to get up. For example, I might spin on the floor, step out with my feet and finish standing with a reach before I do my next move.

Variation

Often a way to grow a movement is to vary it. This involves taking one movement and doing it in many different ways.

For example, if you have created a movement that involves a turn, a reach up high with arms, rising on tip toes and then swinging the arms down, here are three ways that you could develop or vary it:

1. Spin on your knees, reach both arms forward and bring them down.

2. Wrap your arms round your waist to the right. Then wrap to the left, reach forward and up with your right hand and then drop it down.

3. Draw a circle with your foot on the floor. Lift that foot up and straighten it forward. Reach the arm on the same side back, stretching it out and then dropping it back down.

ABOUT THE AUTHOR

Anna Gilderson is a dancer, teacher, choreographer and writer. Her passion is to teach and share her knowledge about the interaction between dance and movement and how that exploration helps us to have a deeper conversation with God.

Anna is mum to two crazy children and wife to an RAF crewman, which means a lot of the time she's juggling business, family and military deployments. However, the wealth of knowledge she has learnt through leaning on God during those times has made her stronger.

Dance and movement have always been a part of her life. The journey it has allowed her to go on has enabled her to grow stronger in her faith, relationships, business and as a person.

Over 10 years ago she started UC Grace, over a simple desire to just share what God gave her. As she began that journey, she learnt a lot about how God speaks to her, how God uses her to speak to others and how when you truly let the Holy Spirit step in to lead a workshop, it always makes you go "wow!"

Putting time in for other passions is integral to how she leads life – sewing for pleasure, making clothes and sewing to create dancing resources such as flags, streamers and ribbons; reading books about prayer, faith and everyday living; putting pen to paper and starting to write for herself; putting together resource books and training manuals to help others; creating dance and movement prayer devotionals and numerous blog posts to encourage others in their journeys of faith – whether that's through movement or not.

Her ultimate passion is sharing how you can deepen your faith through movement and dance. For her, the connection of faith and dance is synonymous in the way that she lives life. Whether people realise it or not, the relationship between movement and faith exists in everyone's everyday.

Opening our Bible to read, bowing our head in prayer, raising our hand in worship, kneeling to take a pause to remember – they are all movements ingrained in you without knowing.

Anna's heart's purpose is to help others recognise that those movements can create a deeper relationship with God.

In essence, she loves encouraging, growing and releasing others to their full potential using dance and movement. Dance is her go-to to connect with God and draw closer to Him. If she's offered the chance to introduce others to this possibility, she jumps, with both feet, into the deep puddle and lets God lead!

ABOUT UC GRACE

UC Grace is a dance company passionate about sharing ways of putting Jesus front and centre in life and generating deeper conversations with God, which together enable people to find grace in their everyday life.

This is done by:

- Encouraging creativity and movement in people's conversations with God.
- Growing people's movement and faith to deepen their conversations with God.
- Releasing people to share how their movement can impact their faith.

UC Grace runs dance mornings, trainings and dance weekends for all levels of ability. It also provides both practical and written resources to help people go deeper with God and develop their leadership skills. These values encase what we do and why we do it. Each value helps us walk with you, your faith and your dance on your journey.

The Christian Faith

This underpins all that we do, putting Jesus central, sharing inspiring Bible verses, passages and blog posts that generate conversations.

Encouragement

Taking the time to encourage each person in who they are, providing training and advice, a listening ear and empathy.

Creativity

A passion to pass on our knowledge, skills and mindset by going outside the box, through various events and trainings and by challenging the use of resources across the arts.

Development

Providing opportunities to develop dance techniques, interaction of movement, faith foundation and skills, by supporting, praying and growing people.

Sharing

Dance, faith, prayer and movement is fun! We LOVE sharing and creating memories through teaching, videos, blog posts and more. Allowing movement to bless others and be blessed through movement ourselves.

If you'd like to explore more, take a look at the UC Grace blog. There is lots of information that allows you to develop what you are passionate about.

www.ucgrace.co.uk/Blog

UC Grace regularly runs both online and in-person training and development days. If you'd like us to work alongside you to develop something, then please get in touch.

We would love to know how this book has impacted your journey of faith, movement and prayer. So please do get in touch and let us know.

www.ucgrace.co.uk

Facebook: @ucgracedance

Instagram: @uc.grace

Lightning Source UK Ltd.
Milton Keynes UK
UKHW021844290322
400786UK00004B/8